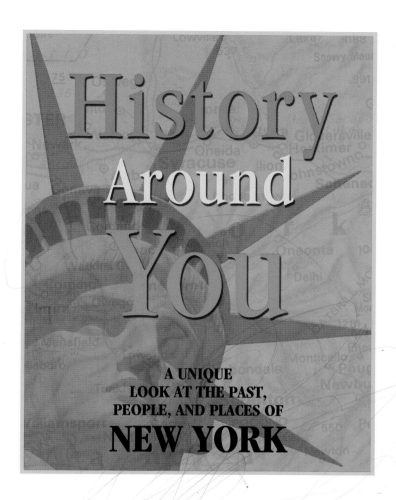

History Around You

A UNIQUE LOOK AT THE PAST, PEOPLE, AND PLACES OF
NEW YORK

Elaine Pascoe

BLACKBIRCH PRESS

An imprint of Thomson Gale, a part of The Thomson Corporation

THOMSON
GALE

Detroit • New York • San Francisco • San Diego • New Haven, Conn. • Waterville, Maine • London • Munich

For more information, contact
Thomson Gale
27500 Drake Rd.
Farmington Hills, MI 48331-3535
Or you can visit our Internet site at http://www.gale.com

Photo credits: Corel: All images: Blackbirch Archives: pages 4, 26, 37, 51 ,52, 63, 66, 67, 68;
Bettmann / CORBIS: page 21, 22, 25, 28, 33, 35, 38, 44, 45, 47, 48, 59, 60; Bob Krist / CORBIS:
pages 32, 69; CORBIS: page 55; Corel Library: page 75; David Ball / CORBIS: page 56; Denver
Public Library: page 54; Giraudon / Art Resource, NY: page 16; Library of Congress: pages 15,
36, 40, 50, 61; Museum of the American Indian: page 10; The New York Public Library: pages 7,
9, 11, 12, 46; The New York Public Library / Art Resource, NY: pages 19, 23; National Portrait
Gallery, Smithsonian Institution / Art Resource, NY: pages 49, 53, 57, 58; North Wind Picture
Archive: pages 14, 30, 31, 39, 41; Photos.com 2004: pages 1, 20, 56, 71, 73; Ray Stubblebine /
Rueters / Landov: page 71; Reuters / CORBIS: page 70; Rick Maiman / Bloomberg News. / Lan-
dov: page 72; Rufus F. Folkks / CORBIS: page 65; Stapleton Collection/Corbis: page 18; Stone /
Getty Images: page 64; Taxi / Getty Images: page 62;

LIBRARY OF CONGRESS CATALOGING-IN-PUBLICATION DATA

Pascoe, Elaine
  History around you: A unique look at New York's past, people, and places / by Elaine Pascoe.
     p. cm. — (History Around You)
  Includes bibliographical references.
  ISBN 1-4103-0490-6 (hardback : alk. paper) Student's Edition
  ISBN 1-4103-0489-2 (paperback : alk. paper) Teacher's Edition
  1. New York (N.Y.)—History—ca. 1600-Present—Juvenile literature. 2. New York (N.Y.)—
Social life and customs— Juvenile literature. [1. New York (N.Y.)—History—ca. 1600-Present. 2.
New York (N.Y.)—Social life and customs] I. Title. II. (Blackbirch Press)

CONTENTS

INTRODUCTION

George Washington, the first U.S. president, gave New York its nickname: the Empire State. He thought of New York as the center of a new American empire. More than two hundred years have passed since Washington's day, and New York has lived up to its name. It has led the nation in business, politics, arts, and many other fields.

New York's location has helped it grow. The state reaches from the Great Lakes in the west to the Atlantic Ocean in the southeast. It is the only state that touches both the Atlantic and the Great Lakes.

Within its borders, the state has a bit of everything. It has the largest city in the United States, New York City. It has farms and forests. It has mountains—the Catskills and the Adirondacks. And it has lakes, ponds, streams, and rivers. The Hudson River is the most important river. It runs from the Adirondack Mountains to the Atlantic Ocean. New York Bay, at the mouth of the Hudson, is a great natural harbor.

In colonial days, these features brought many people to New York. Since then, people have come to the state from all over the world. In this book, you will read their stories.

FOCUS ON:

NEW YORK'S STATE SEAL

The state seal was adopted in 1778. It shows two ships on a river with a grassy shore. In the background is a mountain range, with the sun rising behind it.

The figure of Liberty stands on the left side of the seal. Justice stands on the right. A globe and an American eagle top the seal. The banner below shows the state motto—"Excelsior"—which means *ever upward*.

NEW YORK AT A GLANCE

Location: northeastern U.S.

Neighbors: Canada to the north; Vermont, Massachusetts, and Connecticut to the east; New Jersey to the south; Pennsylvania to the south and west

Capital: Albany

Population: 18,976,457 (2000 census)

Land area: 47,224 sq. mi. (122,310 km); rank, 30th

Highest point: Mount Marcy, 5,344 ft. (1,629 m)

Lowest point: sea level, at the Atlantic Ocean

Largest lake: Oneida, about 80 sq. mi. (207 km)

Longest river: Hudson, 315 mi. (507 km)

Motto: "Excelsior" (*Ever Upward*)

Nickname: Empire State

State bird: bluebird

State flower: rose

State tree: sugar maple

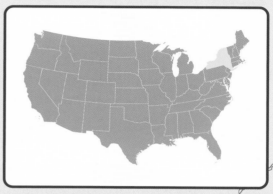

CANADA

Lake Huron

Potsdam

Lake Placid

NEW YORK

VERMONT

NEW HAMPSHIRE

MAINE

Lake Ontario

Oneida Lake

Glens Falls

Niagara Falls   Rochester   Rome

Schenectady

Mohawk River

Buffalo   Geneva   Syracuse

Warsaw   Cooperstown   **Albany**

Ithaca

Mayville   Belmont   Binghamton

MASSACHUSETTS

Kingston

Hudson River

CONNECTICUT

Lake Erie

PENNSYLVANIA

RHODE ISLAND

Yonkers

STATE OF NEW YORK

New York City

Long Island

NEW JERSEY

UNIT 1 | NEW YORK'S FIRST PEOPLE

Suppose you could travel back in time to the year 1500. The area that is now New York State was covered by forests then. Black bears, deer, moose, and other animals roamed the woodlands. Fish thrived in the clear lakes and rivers.

There were people, too. They were American Indians. Their ancestors reached North America more than ten thousand years ago. These first people crossed from Asia over a **land bridge** that has since slipped under the ocean. Over thousands of years, they spread throughout the Americas.

In 1500, several Indian tribes lived in the New York area. They are usually divided into two main groups, the Iroquois and the Algonquians, based on differences in their language and **culture.**

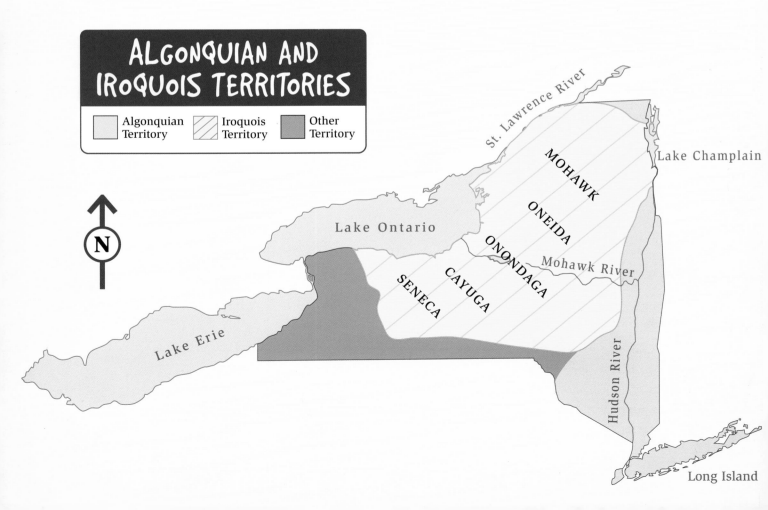

ALGONQUIAN AND IROQUOIS TERRITORIES

Algonquian Territory   Iroquois Territory   Other Territory

N

St. Lawrence River
Lake Champlain
MOHAWK
ONEIDA
Lake Ontario
ONONDAGA
Mohawk River
CAYUGA
SENECA
Lake Erie
Hudson River
Long Island

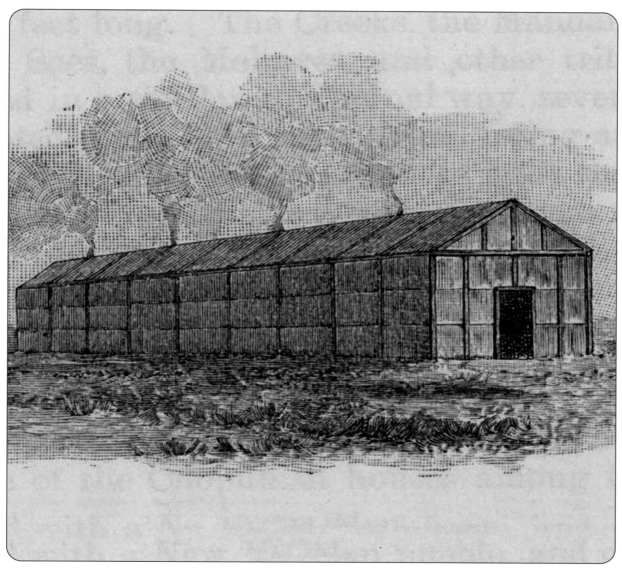

The Iroquios longhouse was a wood and bark structure up to two hundred feet in length. It was home to as many as twenty Iroquois families at a time.

PEOPLE OF THE LONGHOUSE

Sometime before the mid-1500s, five tribes banded together to form what became known as the Iroquois **Confederacy**. They were the Cayuga, Mohawk, Oneida, Onondaga, and Seneca tribes. Later a sixth tribe, the Tuscarora, joined. Together, these tribes controlled much of northern and western New York.

The Iroquois lived in hilltop villages. They called themselves the Haudenosaunee—in English, people of the longhouse. An Iroquois longhouse was a dwelling up to two hundred feet long. The house was framed with wood poles and then covered with tree bark. There was a door at each end. Smoke holes were spaced along the arched roof, with hearths for cooking fires directly below.

FOCUS ON:

HIAWATHA

Iroquois legends honor Hiawatha (an Onondaga) as the founder of the Iroquois Confederacy. The stories say that Hiawatha and Deganawidah (a Huron) grew tired of the wars that raged between tribes. The two men went from tribe to tribe, asking each group to form a peace alliance. One by one, four other tribes joined with the Onondaga to form the confederacy.

There are different versions of this story. Historians are not sure when this happened or even when Hiawatha lived. Some believe it was as early as the 1100s. Others think it was much later.

The poet Henry Wadsworth Longfellow added to the confusion about Hiawatha. In 1855, he wrote a poem called *The Song of Hiawatha* The hero of the poem was called Hiawatha. But Longfellow based the story on an Algonquian legend about a different hero.

Up to twenty families might live in a longhouse. Each family had its own space. The families who lived together in this way were all members of the same **clan**. They were related through their mothers to a common ancestor. Each clan had an animal symbol—bear, wolf, or turtle, for example.

Women headed the clans. Women owned property. And when a man

What would it be like to share a home with twenty families?

married, he moved to his wife's longhouse. Their children became members of her clan.

Leaders of each Iroquois tribe met in **councils** to decide important matters such as when to go to war. The council leaders were called **sachems**. They were men, but they were always chosen by the women.

IROQUOIS LIFE

Iroquois men and women had clear roles. Women were farmers. They planted corn, beans, and squash in fields cleared from the forest. Children worked and played alongside their mothers as they tended the fields.

In spring, women drew sap from maple trees and boiled it to make maple sugar. In summer, women and children went into the forest to gather nuts, berries, roots, and greens. During the warm months of the year, the people of the longhouse had to grow and gather enough food to last through the cold winter. Food was preserved by drying and stored in a special area at one end of the longhouse.

Men helped clear farm fields, but they did not plant or tend crops. They were hunters. Their main quarry was deer. The men often worked together to drive many deer into a trap, where hunters waited with bows and arrows or spears.

They also hunted bear and wild turkey and other birds. They snared small animals such as muskrat, beaver, and porcupine. And they

Tribal council leaders, called sachems, decide important matters for the tribe. Though sachems are men, they are chosen by the women of the tribe.

fished, mainly using nets and spears. In winter, when lakes and ponds froze, they cut holes in the ice to catch fish.

Men were also warriors. The Iroquois fought with neighboring groups, including the Algonquian tribes. In battle, men wore armor made of wood slats as protection against arrows.

THE ALGONQUIANS

Algonquian is not the name of a single tribe. The term refers to people who spoke any of several Algonquian languages. Dozens of different American Indian tribes used these languages.

Several Algonquian tribes lived in the southern part of the New York area. The Mohicans (or Mahicans) were the largest group. They lived along the Hudson River and east into New England. The Lenni Lenapes lived west of the Mohicans, near the start of the Delaware River. The Shinnecocks lived on Long Island.

The ways of these tribes were not very different from the ways of the Iroquois. Like the Iroquois, the Algonquian tribes relied on the natural world for everything. The forest trees provided wood and bark for their homes and canoes. Plants provided food and medicines. Animals of the forest provided meat and much more.

FOCUS ON:

FALSE-FACE MASKS

The Iroquois believed that spirits could drive off sickness and other evils. Through dances and ceremonies, they called on spirits to help the sick. The people who performed these rituals were medicine men, and they formed several different medicine societies.

The best known was the False Face Society. Members of this society wore wooden masks called false-face masks. The masks were carved from tree trunks, and each was thought to capture the spirit in that tree. No two masks were the same. But they all shared one feature: a crooked nose.

Iroquois medicine men made false-face masks believed to hold spirits of trees.

Algonquian life was recorded by travelers through the tribal lands. Many drawings of manners, customs, weapons and clothing show us what life was like for the Algonquian hundreds of years ago.

Hides became clothing. Bones were shaped into tools. Guts and sinews became thread and string.

In their villages, some Mohicans lived in longhouses, like the Iroquois. But many built smaller homes, called *wikkums* or wigwams. These homes were round, with domed roofs. The frames were made of saplings, bent and tied together at the top. They were covered with hides or bark to keep out the wind and rain. Except for the door, a smoke hole at the top was the only opening.

Mohican women cared for the home, children, and gardens. Men were hunters and warriors. Many Mohicans lived along rivers or near the ocean, and they were great fishermen. They netted or speared herring, shad, trout, and other fish. Fish that was not eaten right away was smoked and stored for winter in pits lined with bark or grass. Meat and vegetables were dried and stored for winter in the same way.

HONORING NATURE

Because they lived so close to nature, American Indians had great respect for

DID YOU KNOW . . .

Place names are a reminder of New York's first people. Many towns, counties, lakes, and other features are named for tribes that lived in the state. Others take their names from Indian words. Here are some of those names, with the meanings of the Indian words from which they come.

Adirondack (mountains): Bark eater or porcupine

Cattaraugus (town, county): Bad smelling banks (for the smell of natural gas leaking from rock seams)

Chautauqua (town, county, lake): Where the fish was taken out

Chemung (county): Big horn (from the name of a Delaware Indian village)

Chenango (town, county, river): Large bullthistle (a plant)

Oswego (town, county, river): The out-pouring (for the mouth of the river)

Otsego (lake): Place of the rock

Saranac (lake): Cluster of stars

Schenectady (city, county): On the other side of the pine lands

Schoharie (county, reservoir): Floating driftwood

Tioga (county): At the forks (for what was once an important Indian meeting place)

Wyoming (town, county): Broad bottomlands

Native Americans set up saplings that form the frame for their wigwams. They covered the frames with hides or bark to keep out wind and rain.

THINK ABOUT IT!

Why was nature important to the American Indians?

its power. Both the Iroquois and the Algonquian tribes honored the spirits they believed shaped and controlled the natural world.

The Iroquois marked important times of year with celebrations. Festivals celebrated planting in spring and harvests in summer and fall. The biggest event was the Midwinter Festival, held after the last big hunt of the year. It included feasting, dances, and games. One of those games was the forerunner of the modern sport of lacrosse.

The Algonquian way of life also followed the rhythm of the seasons. In early spring, the people would camp out in stands of sugar maples to collect sap from the trees and boil it to make sugar. Making maple sugar was an important ceremony and a way to welcome spring.

Other ceremonies marked planting and harvesttimes. During winter, people gathered around their fires. They made and repaired the tools, containers, clothing, and other items they used all year. And they told old stories that had been passed down from one generation to the next.

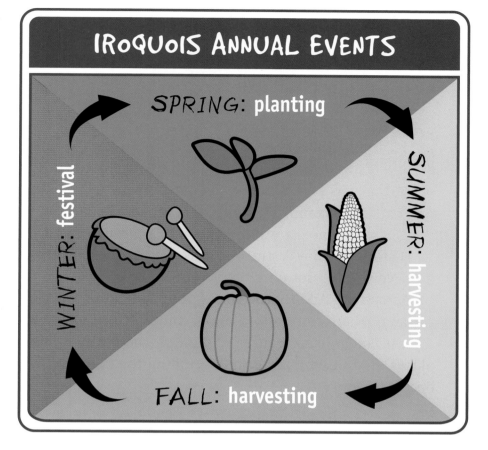

IROQUOIS ANNUAL EVENTS

SPRING: planting

SUMMER: harvesting

FALL: harvesting

WINTER: festival

CHAPTER REVIEW

1. How many tribes first formed the Iroquois Confederacy?
2. What is a longhouse?
3. What was the main job of an Iroquois woman?
4. Where did the Mohicans live?
5. What was the most important Iroquois festival?

UNIT 2 | EUROPEANS ARRIVE

In 1524, the Indians who lived near the mouth of the Hudson River watched as a strange sailing ship entered New York Bay. The ship was *La Dauphine*. Its captain was the Italian explorer Giovanni da Verrazano. The king of France had sent him to find the Northwest Passage—a water route across North America to Asia.

Historians think Verrazano was the first European to reach the region that is now New York. But other explorers would follow.

Across the Atlantic Ocean, European countries were growing strong. France, England, the Netherlands, Spain, and Portugal were competing for riches from distant lands. Each wanted to control trade routes. Their ships were sailing to places all around the world—including the corner of North America that would become New York.

Henry Hudson's ship, the Half Moon, is seen here sailing up the river named after Hudson. Explorers such as Hudson brought change to the Native American's way of life.

FOCUS ON:

HENRY HUDSON (DIED 1611)

Henry Hudson was an English explorer. History does not tell much about his early life. In 1607, an English company hired him to find a short route from Europe to Asia by sailing north to the Arctic. He made two tries, but pack ice forced him to turn back.

The Dutch backed his third voyage in April 1609. His ship, the *Half Moon*, was just sixty feet (18.3 m) long and had a crew of eighteen men. Again, he sailed north and met ice. But this time he turned the ship west and headed across the Atlantic Ocean. He hoped to find a water route across North America to the Pacific Ocean.

Hudson reached New York Bay in September. He sailed more than 150 miles (240 km) up the river that now bears his name. But as the river grew shallower, he realized it was not the water route he sought.

Hudson's fourth voyage was his last. In April 1610, he set out in an English ship, the *Discovery*. Sailing north and west, he reached what is today Hudson Bay in northern Canada. Then winter came. His ship was icebound in the frozen water. The crew suffered from cold, hunger, and disease.

In spring, Hudson wanted to continue west. But the crew wanted to go home. The crew set Hudson and a few men loyal to him adrift in a small boat. They were never seen again.

Henry Hudson (standing, left) met Native Americans as he sailed up the river that now bears his name.

EARLY EXPLORERS

Verrazano did not stay in New York for long. He noted the mighty river that emptied into the bay. Then he sailed on, up the coast of North America. Henry Hudson, an Englishman working for the Dutch, was the first European to explore that river. It now bears his name.

In 1609, Hudson sailed his ship *Half Moon* up the river as far as present-day Albany. His men traded and fought with the Indians they met. Hudson, too, was looking for the Northwest Passage. He did not find it, but he claimed the region for the Dutch.

At about the same time, the French explorer Samuel de Champlain reached northern New York. Champlain had founded a fur-trading post at Quebec. He formed alliances with Huron and Ottawa Indians, who were bitter enemies of the Iroquois.

Samuel de Champlain fought the Iroquois alongside the Huron and the Ottawa in northern New York.

In 1609, Champlain joined a war party of Huron and Ottawa traveling south to fight the Iroquois. They met the enemy on the shore of the lake in northern New York that is now named for Champlain. Champlain and his men shot several Iroquois. The fight made the Iroquois lasting enemies of the French.

These early events were the first signs of great changes to come. Before long, people from three continents—America, Europe, and Africa—would come together in New York.

THE DUTCH ARRIVE

The *Half Moon* sailed back to the Netherlands with glowing reports of a land rich in fur-bearing animals. Soon more Dutch ships sailed for North America.

Among the explorers was Adriaen Block, who sailed along coastal New York and southern New England in 1613 and 1614. Block's ship, the *Tiger*, was lost in New York Bay. He and his crew built huts and a new ship, the *Restless*. In it, Block explored the coast of Long Island.

The Dutch set up a trading post, Fort Nassau, near present-day Albany, in 1614. A few years later, Dutch merchants formed the West India Company. The Dutch government gave this company the sole right to trade in North America. The region around the

THINK ABOUT IT!
Why did most early colonists settle along rivers?

DID YOU KNOW . . .

The Dutch colony of New Amsterdam lasted only about forty years. But Dutch influence has lasted much longer. We still eat Dutch foods, such as waffles, and play Dutch sports, like bowling. Dutch building styles such as double "Dutch" doors are still seen.

Many places in New York have Dutch names. The colonists often named their settlements after towns in their homeland. Other names came from Dutch words and the names of settlers. Here are some of them:

Bowery (section of New York City): For the farm (*bouwerij*) owned by Peter Stuyvesant

Bronx (borough of New York City): For Jonas Bronck, a settler who had a farm there

Coney Island: Originally Conyne Eylandt, meaning "rabbit island"

Catskill (mountains and town): Originally Kats Kil, meaning "cats stream"

Rensselaer (city and county): For Kiliaen Van Rensselaer, a wealthy patroon

Spuyten Duyvil (section of New York City): "Devil's spout," for dangerous currents in part of the Harlem River

Yonkers (city): For Jonkheer Adriaen Van der Donck, an early settler in the area

Hudson River, which the Dutch called the North River, became a **colony** called New Netherland. In 1624, the first settlers arrived.

The Dutch West India Company controlled the fur trade. It controlled nearly everything else in New Netherland, too. The company sent settlers to several places. The two most important settlements were Fort Orange (now Albany) and New Amsterdam (now New York City). Traders brought furs to the post at Fort Orange. Boats took the furs down

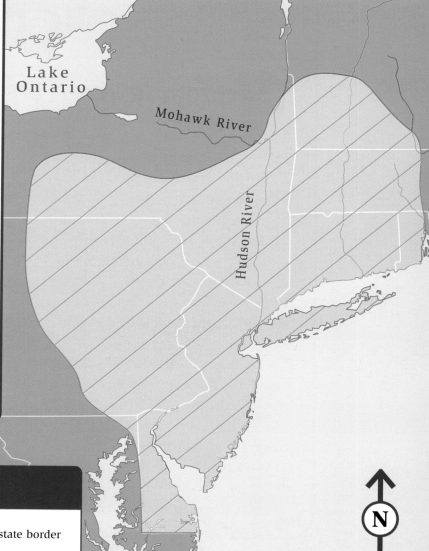

NEW NETHERLAND

▨	Area described as New Netherland in 1636	▨ Modern-day state border

the river to New Amsterdam, at the tip of Manhattan Island. Then Dutch merchant ships carried them to Europe.

To bring more people to New Netherland, the Dutch handed out huge tracts of land to people called patroons (patrons). Patroons had only to send fifty settlers and put up the money to buy the land from the Indians. The amount was never large. Peter Minuit, the governor of the new colony, bought Manhattan Island from the Indians who lived there for trade goods worth about twenty-four dollars.

EUROPEANS AND THE INDIANS

The Mohicans and other Indians may have seen these land sales differently than the Dutch did. In Indian cultures, people did not own real estate. Instead, a group would use an area of land for a time. When the soil became poor after several growing seasons, a whole village would move to a new place. The Indians may have thought they were giving the Dutch the right to share the land and use it in this way.

FOCUS ON:

THE NORTHWEST PASSAGE

European ships first sailed across the Atlantic Ocean hoping to find a fast route to the silks, spices, and other riches of Asia. But America blocked the way. Ships had to sail all the way around the tip of South America to reach the Pacific Ocean and Asian lands.

Europeans were sure that there must be a water route across North America. They searched for years for this fabled Northwest Passage. The search brought the first explorers to New York.

But the Northwest Passage was not found until the 1800s—and it turned out to be useless. The route runs through Canada's northern islands, the Arctic Ocean, and the Bering Strait. Ice blocks it for much of the year.

A ship cuts through the ice in search of the Northwest Passage.

This painting shows New Netherland governor Peter Minuit buying the island of Manhattan from the Indians who lived there.

The coming of Europeans changed life for the Indians in many ways. Trade brought guns, which helped them hunt. It brought metal tools, iron kettles, and many other items that they had not seen before. In time, these items replaced traditional handmade goods.

Traders also supplied the Indians with liquor. Alcohol use became a terrible problem in some tribes. Even more serious were diseases—smallpox, measles, and others—that Europeans brought. Because Indians had never been around these diseases, they did not have a natural ability to fight them. Thousands of Indians died in outbreaks of disease. Sometimes whole villages were wiped out.

THINK ABOUT IT!

Was the fur trade good or bad for American Indians? Why?

FOCUS ON:

FUR FOR HATS

New York's forests were filled with foxes, otters, and many other fur-bearing animals. But Europeans especially wanted beaver pelts. The pelts were used to make felt for hats.

Felt is a cloth made from pressed animal hair. It is waterproof. It can be molded easily, and it wears well. All that makes it great for hats. From the 1600s to the 1800s beaver hats were the height of men's fashion in Europe. The need for beaver pelts was endless. And North America was the main source of the pelts.

Felt hats made from beaver furs were popular in Europe for almost two hundred years.

Meanwhile, Indian tribes competed for the fur trade. That caused trouble between groups such as the Mohicans and Mohawks. Indians were also caught up in conflicts between the Dutch, the English, and the French, who all wanted to control the fur trade. As more Europeans arrived, the demand for land grew, and tensions rose.

Colonists clashed with Indians, and some of the clashes turned into small wars. In time, the Mohicans were driven from much of their land. They moved east into what is now Connecticut.

SLAVES IN NEW NETHERLAND

The Dutch were already in the slave trade when they founded New Netherland. Dutch ships took slaves from the coast of West Africa to work on **plantations** in South America and the Caribbean Islands. The first African slaves arrived in New Netherland not long after the first Dutch settlers.

Most of the slaves were brought from the Caribbean. They helped build the new settlements, including a fort at New Amsterdam. They worked on farms and did many other jobs.

The Dutch West India Company owned the slaves. Some slaves gained their freedom after many years of service. They received small plots of land to farm. Thus, by the mid-1600s, there were a few free blacks in the colony.

THE ENGLISH TAKE OVER

Dutch merchants grew rich in the fur trade. But the Dutch West India Company struggled to keep the colony going. The patroon system was not successful. Few settlers wanted to come when the land was owned by a handful of wealthy individuals. The Dutch changed the rules so that more people could own land. Even so, nearby English, French, and Swedish colonies grew faster.

New Amsterdam had a lively mixture of people from all over Europe.

They enjoyed religious freedom and other liberties. But the settlement was poorly governed. It had lots of taverns, but no schools or hospitals. Pigs and other farm animals roamed the unpaved streets.

A new governor, Peter Stuyvesant, arrived in 1647. He tried to solve New Amsterdam's problems. He was strict and unpopular, but the colony began

New Amsterdam's location on the Island of Manhattan at the mouth of the Hudson River made it an important port to the Dutch, English, and French.

to thrive. Then conflict between England and the Netherlands ended Dutch rule.

The British had long had an eye on the Dutch colony. They knew that New Amsterdam's location at the mouth of the Hudson River made it an important port. They also did not want Dutch settlements between the English colonies of Virginia and Massachusetts.

In 1664, English warships entered New York Harbor. Their goal was to drive the Dutch from North America. Stuyvesant was forced to surrender.

FOCUS ON: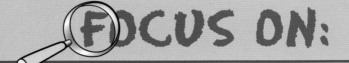

PETER STUYVESANT (1592—1672)

Peter Stuyvesant was the last governor of New Netherland. He was a colorful figure, known for his strict rule and hot temper. People called him "old silver leg" because he wore a peg leg ringed with silver bands. He had lost his right leg in a battle.

Stuyvesant was just the man to bring order to New Amsterdam. He banned the sale of alcohol to Indians. He founded the settlement's first fire department, school, jail, and market. He had streets paved and forts repaired. The colony thrived. But his strict laws made him unpopular.

When English warships arrived at New Amsterdam in 1664, Stuyvesant was prepared to fight them. The settlers begged him not to. The English had promised that the Dutch could keep their farms and businesses if they surrendered.

The English lived up to their word. Stuyvesant lived out his days on his farm in what became New York.

Peter Stuyvesant established order in New Netherland by enacting strict laws.

In this painting, Peter Stuyvesant surrenders New Amsterdam to the English, who renamed the town New York.

King Charles II of England gave control of the colony to James, the Duke of York and of Albany, who would later become King James II. In his honor, New Amsterdam became New York City, and Fort Orange became Albany.

CHAPTER REVIEW

1. Who was the first European to reach New York Bay?
2. What country did Samuel de Champlain come from?
3. Where did the Mohicans go when they were forced from their lands?
4. Who owned the first slaves in New Netherland?
5. Who was Peter Stuyvesant?

BRITISH NEW YORK

New York thrived under British rule. Settlers spread along the Hudson north of Albany and west into the Mohawk Valley. Albany and New York City grew quickly. In 1664 there were just 9,000 people in all of New York. In 1771, on the eve of the American Revolution, there were 168,000.

The Hudson River helped the colony grow. It carried furs, farm goods, and lumber from Albany and other points to New York City. From there ships took goods to Britain or its colonies in the West Indies. Ships came back from the West Indies with rum, molasses, and sugar. From Britain they brought glassware, cutlery, expensive fabrics, and other goods.

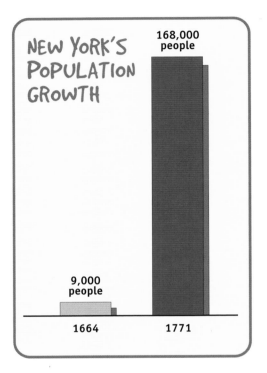

NEW YORK'S POPULATION GROWTH

168,000 people

9,000 people

1664   1771

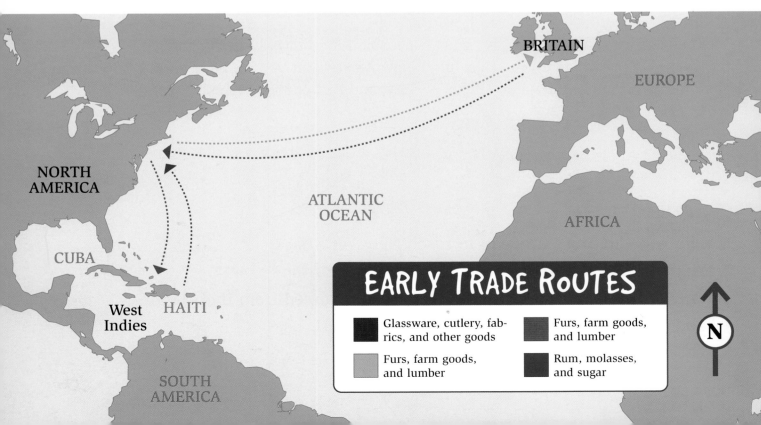

EARLY TRADE ROUTES

- Glassware, cutlery, fabrics, and other goods
- Furs, farm goods, and lumber
- Furs, farm goods, and lumber
- Rum, molasses, and sugar

BRITAIN

EUROPE

NORTH AMERICA

ATLANTIC OCEAN

AFRICA

CUBA

West Indies

HAITI

SOUTH AMERICA

N

FOCUS ON:

COLONIAL SCHOOLS

The Dutch set up schools that were open to all in many New Netherland communities. Under English rule, most of these schools closed. Instead, there were private academies and private tutors for the children of wealthy families. In other families, parents taught their children as best they could.

Some children learned to read at dame schools. These were schools taught by women in their own homes. Sometimes families got together to hire a teacher. They might build a small school. But often the teacher would travel from house to house, teaching children in different families each day.

Paper was scarce and costly. Students wrote on slates, with chalk. Books were scarce, too. Children learned their ABC's from hornbooks. These were paddle-shaped boards that held a sheet of printed paper. A clear cover made from animal horn protected the paper.

Colonial children used hornbooks to learn the alphabet.

By law, the colonists were not supposed to trade with any country other than Britain. Many people ignored the law. New York City became a haven for smugglers and pirates.

DAILY LIFE

Most of New York's early settlers farmed land that they rented from big landowners. Life was hard for these farmers and their families. They had to grow or make almost everything they needed.

Families worked together to get everything done. They grew field crops such as oats, corn, hay, and flax, which was spun to make linen. They planted apple orchards and gathered the fruit. Their vegetable gardens were filled with turnips, parsnips, onions, and squash. They raised cows, sheep, and pigs. They preserved meat by salting or pickling it, and they tanned hides to make leather. They gathered firewood and stored it for winter.

THINK ABOUT IT!

What was it like to grow up on a colonial farm? Would you have liked that life?

Women sewed clothing and linens for the family. They made soap, butter, and candles. They dried apples and other fruits to preserve them for winter. They also cooked meals, cleaned the house, washed and ironed clothes, and did dozens of other chores.

Most families had lots of children. The children were expected to pitch in. They carried water from the well. They stacked firewood. They fed the chickens and did many other jobs. Often

The job of a blacksmith was to forge iron. Blacksmiths made household items and repaired wagons and carts.

DID YOU KNOW . . .

Many New York towns were laid out in colonial times. In Smithtown, on Long Island, a colorful legend tells how the borders were set.

According to the tale, an English settler named Richard Smith made a deal with local Indians in 1665. They agreed to let him keep as much land as he could circle in a day while riding his bull, Whisper. Smith picked the longest day of the year to make the ride. Whisper covered a total of fifty-five miles that day, enclosing what became Smithtown.

There is no truth to the legend, historians say. But the story of the Smithtown Bull is fun. Today a bronze statue of Whisper stands in Smithtown, honoring the legend.

children had to keep a fire going in the family hearth. Fires had to be kept burning all year, even in the hot summer, for cooking.

With so much work to do, there was not much time for fun. But families met at church services each week. Women held sewing and quilting bees, where they chatted as they worked together.

In towns and cities, people had more chances to get together. They were also able to buy more products. By the 1700s many trades were thriving in New York. Most towns had a **grist-mill**, a **sawmill**, and a blacksmith.

In larger towns, shoemakers, cabinet-makers, clockmakers, metalsmiths, and other **artisans** set up shop. Boys often worked as **apprentices** in their work-shops. The boys learned a trade. And they helped their families make ends meet.

Wealthy merchants, landowners, and officials lived well in colonial New York. They could afford to buy goods from England. They could also afford servants and slaves.

SERVANTS AND SLAVES

Workers were always needed in the colony. Many newcomers arrived in New York as **indentured servants**. In exchange for passage to America, they agreed to serve for a certain period of time, often seven years. After that, they were free to seek other work.

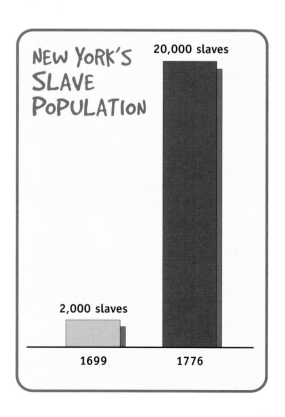

NEW YORK'S SLAVE POPULATION

20,000 slaves

2,000 slaves

1699   1776

Slaves also helped fill the need for workers. There were more than two thousand African slaves in New York at the end of the 1600s. By the time of the American Revolution, there were almost twenty thousand slaves.

Slavery in New York was not like slavery in the South. There, plantation owners kept hundreds of slaves to work their fields. New York slave owners generally had no more than a dozen slaves. Most had only one or two. Slaves worked in the fields alongside their owners. Some learned

The Dutch were the first to bring African slaves to New York (pictured), and slavery continued under the British.

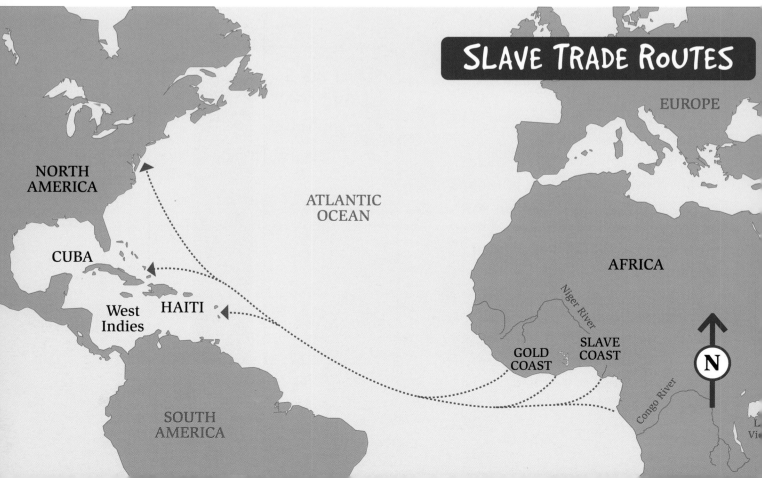

SLAVE TRADE ROUTES

MARY JEMISON (1743—1833)

In 1758, when she was about fifteen years old, Mary Jemison was captured by Shawnee Indians who raided her family's home in Pennsylvania. Her family was killed. The Shawnee sold her to the Seneca, who adopted her. They gave her the name Dehgewanus. Dehgewanus married and went with her husband and their young son to Seneca territory along the Genesee River in western New York. Her husband died on the journey, but she finished the trip on her own. She remarried and had seven more children.

Dehgewanus was given a chance to return to white society, but she chose to stay with the Senecas for the rest of her life. She told her story to the writer James Seaver, who published *The Life and Times of Mrs. Mary Jemison* in 1824.

skills such as shoemaking and woodworking. Women slaves were often household servants.

Strict rules governed the slaves' lives. For example, slaves could not gather in groups of more than three. If they broke rules, they could be whipped. A slave revolt in 1712 was harshly put down.

TROUBLE WITH FRANCE

In the late 1600s, rivalry grew between Britain and France. Each country wanted to control North America. They fought four wars in North America, one right after the other, from 1689 to 1759.

New York, because it was close to French Canada, saw many battles. The British and the Iroquois were allies in the fight. They used New York as a base for attacks on French territory. The French and their Indian allies often attacked British frontier settlements. In 1690, French and Indian raiders destroyed Schenectady.

The last war began in 1754. It is known as the French and Indian War or Seven Years' War. At first the British suffered many setbacks. Fort Oswego fell to the French in 1756. But the British rallied and won the war in 1759.

During the trouble with France, New York's frontier was a dangerous place. Few new settlers arrived. After the fighting ended, more people came. But New Yorkers would soon face new problems.

SEEDS OF THE REVOLUTION

Fighting France was costly for Britain. After the fighting ended, the British decided to raise money by taxing the colonies. The colonists had no say in these new taxes. Many colonists were angry. "No taxation without **representation**," they cried.

FOCUS ON:

A PLAN OF UNION

The Albany Congress met in Albany from June 19 to July 11, 1754. Its main purpose was to strengthen ties between the Iroquois and the colonies. New York, Pennsylvania, Maryland, Massachusetts, Connecticut, Rhode Island, and New Hampshire sent delegates to the meeting. So did the Iroquois.

The meeting is best known for a plan put forward by Benjamin Franklin, of Pennsylvania. He called on the colonies to form a union. They would still be under British rule, but they would have a central government. The union never formed. But Franklin's Albany Plan of Union was a sign of things to come.

Benjamin Franklin encouraged the colonists to unite against British rule.

The Stamp Act of 1765 was especially unpopular. This law taxed newspapers and other printed materials, even playing cards. **Delegates** from nine colonies met in New York City to take action against this tax. They sent a **petition** to Britain. And they agreed to buy no British goods until the tax was ended.

Taxes were not the only reason for anger toward Britain. Colonists were forced to provide housing and food for British soldiers. They did not want to **quarter** soldiers in their homes.

Groups called the Sons of Liberty formed in every colony. In New York City, the Sons of Liberty met at a pine tree they called the "liberty pole." There they led rallies and gave speeches.

The Stamp Act was ended in 1766. But new taxes on tea and other goods replaced it. The colonists opposed these taxes, too. In 1773, Massachusetts colonists protested by dumping a ship's cargo of tea into Boston Harbor. Word of the Boston Tea Party soon reached New York City. Colonists there staged a tea-dumping protest, too.

Colonists dressed as Indians dumped tea into Boston Harbor to protest British taxes. This event became known as the Boston Tea Party.

King George III of Britain was furious at these protests. Britain tried to close the port of Boston and punish Massachusetts in other ways. But the other colonies rallied to the side of Massachusetts.

New Yorkers were among the first to call for a meeting to decide what to do. The First Continental Congress met in September 1774 in Philadelphia, Pennsylvania. John Jay, James Duane,

A reenactment of the American Revolution shows British soldiers in their famous red coats.

JOHN PETER ZENGER (1697–1746)

John Peter Zenger helped establish freedom of the press in America. Zenger was a printer. He founded a newspaper, the *New York Weekly Journal*, in 1733. In it, he criticized the British governor, William Cosby. For that, Zenger was arrested and charged with libel. Andrew Hamilton, the most famous lawyer in the colonies, defended Zenger at his trial in 1735. Hamilton argued that because what Zenger's paper printed was true, he should not be jailed. The jury agreed, and Zenger was freed.

British soldiers oversee the burning of Peter Zenger's Weekly Journal on Wall Street on November 6, 1734.

and Philip Livingston represented New York.

The delegates did not call for independence. They still thought of themselves as loyal British citizens. But they wanted Britain to recognize their rights. They called for an end to harsh laws.

The delegates made plans to meet again the following May. By that time, the Revolutionary War had begun.

CHAPTER REVIEW

1. What did ships bring to New York from the West Indies?
2. What was one job that women did in colonial New York?
3. How did many boys learn trades?
4. How many slaves were in New York at the time of the American Revolution?
5. What was the "liberty pole"?

UNIT 4 | THE REVOLUTIONARY WAR

The Revolutionary War began in Lexington, Massachusetts, on April 19, 1775. There, British soldiers traded shots with a handful of men in the Massachusetts **militia**. The war that followed ended with the founding of a new nation—the United States of America.

New York played a big role in the war because of its location. New York was in the middle of the colonies. By controlling New York, the British hoped to cut off New England from the South.

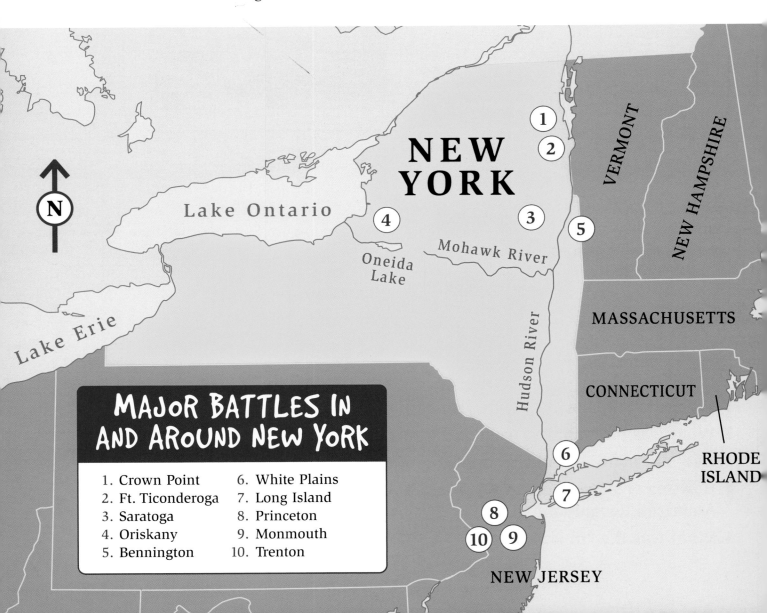

NEW YORK

Lake Ontario

Oneida Lake

Lake Erie

Mohawk River

Hudson River

VERMONT

NEW HAMPSHIRE

MASSACHUSETTS

CONNECTICUT

RHODE ISLAND

NEW JERSEY

N

MAJOR BATTLES IN AND AROUND NEW YORK

1. Crown Point
2. Ft. Ticonderoga
3. Saratoga
4. Oriskany
5. Bennington
6. White Plains
7. Long Island
8. Princeton
9. Monmouth
10. Trenton

NEW YORK'S WAR BEGINS

Just three weeks after the fight at Lexington, the war came to New York. American forces captured the British fort of Ticonderoga, at the southern tip of Lake Champlain.

It was a bold move. A ragtag group called the Green Mountain Boys

DID YOU KNOW . . .

Many places in New York mark important events in the Revolution. Here are a few of them:

Fort Ticonderoga: This restored fort is a national historic site. It hosts military reenactments and other events.

Fraunces Tavern: This historic building in New York City is where George Washington bid farewell to his officers in 1783. Today it is a museum with displays about colonial life.

Saratoga National Historic Park: This park includes the 1777 battlefield. It hosts demonstrations and other events.

Senate House: This simple stone house in Kingston was the first meeting place of the New York senate.

Washington's Headquarters: This farmhouse in Newburgh was George Washington's home and headquarters in 1782–1783. It has displays that show how Washington and his family lived.

FOCUS ON:

NATHAN HALE (1755—1776)

Nathan Hale, a Connecticut schoolteacher, joined the American army soon after the Revolution began. In 1776, he volunteered to slip behind British lines on Long Island as a spy. His goal was to get information about the enemy's strength and plans. But the British caught him and hanged him without a trial. Hale became famous for his last words: "I only regret that I have but one life to lose for my country."

The British hanged Nathan Hale in New York.

marched on the fort. Led by Ethan Allen, they surprised the British soldiers. The Americans took the fort without firing a shot.

Fort Ticonderoga had something the Americans needed badly—cannons. Over the winter of 1775–1776, Americans hauled the fort's big guns to Boston. George Washington, leader of the newly formed Continental army, set them up on hills overlooking that city.

After the Declaration of Independence was read aloud in New York City, patriots toppled a statue of King George III.

With cannons aimed at their troops, the British could not hold Boston. British general William Howe and his soldiers left the city in the spring of 1776.

But Howe did not give up the fight. His forces headed for New York City. If he could take the city, he would have the best port in the colonies. Washington rushed south to defend New York.

In July 1776, the Continental Congress in Philadelphia approved the Declaration of Independence. Washington was in New York City. On July 9, he had the declaration read aloud to the public. That night, a mob of New York City **patriots** pulled down a huge lead statue of King George III. They melted down the statue and used the lead to make bullets.

But some New Yorkers did not want to fight for freedom. They were **loyalists.** They wanted to stay British subjects.

THE STRUGGLE FOR NEW YORK

The British built up their forces around New York. In August 1776, they drove Washington's army from Long Island. Washington pulled back to Manhattan. Then he moved north to White Plains. The British followed him there. He was forced to retreat to New Jersey.

New York City was in British hands. But patriots still held much of the rest of New York. The state adopted its first **constitution** in April 1777. George Clinton, the first elected governor, was sworn in that July. But by then the British had begun a campaign to win all of New York.

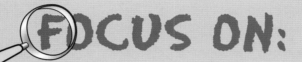

FOCUS ON:

JOHN JAY (1745—1829)

John Jay was a leading statesman in Revolutionary times. A lawyer, he represented New York at the Continental Congress in 1774.

Jay was against independence at first. But once independence was declared, he supported it. With John Adams and Benjamin Franklin, he negotiated the Treaty of Paris, which ended the Revolutionary War.

Later, Jay helped win approval of the U.S. Constitution. He also served as the first chief justice of the U.S. Supreme Court and as governor of New York.

John Jay represented New York at the First Continental Congress.

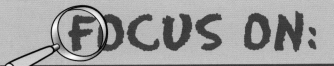

FOCUS ON:

JOSEPH BRANT
(1742–1807)

Joseph Brant was a Mohawk leader during the Revolution. His Mohawk name was Thayendanegea. Brant was a strong supporter of the British. During the Revolution, he led successful attacks on colonists in western New York. An American army finally defeated him, burning many Indian villages. Brant and his followers moved to Canada.

Joseph Brant led the Mohawks during the Revolution.

The British plan was to send three armies into New York. Howe would march up the Hudson River from New York City. General John Burgoyne would march south from Canada along Lake Champlain. A third British force would march east from Lake Ontario. They would all meet in Albany.

The British got off to a good start. Burgoyne took Fort Ticonderoga on July 6, 1777. He marched on toward Albany. But he soon ran into trouble.

Patriots felled trees along the British army's path. This slowed the British march. The British began to run out of food. In August, Burgoyne sent a thousand soldiers to raid American supplies at Bennington, which is now in Vermont. Patriots beat them soundly.

The British met trouble in western New York, too. Americans blocked them at Fort Stanwix, in the Mohawk Valley. The British had to turn back.

SARATOGA: A TURNING POINT

By September, Burgoyne was just north of Albany, near Saratoga. An American army under General Horatio Gates stopped him at Freeman's Farm on September 19. Burgoyne dug in to wait for help. But help did not come. Howe was not marching up the Hudson as planned. He had gone south instead, hoping to take Philadelphia.

Burgoyne finally decided to fight his way through the American forces. The Americans stopped him on October 7. Ten days later, he surrendered at Saratoga.

Saratoga was a huge victory for the Americans. It showed the world that the Americans could beat the British. After this, France and America became allies. France sent ships and soldiers to help the Americans.

Saratoga thus was more than a military victory. It was a turning point in the war.

American general Horatio Gates defeated the British at Saratoga.

THE WAR'S END

After 1777, most of the war's major battles took place south of New York. The British still held New York City. The Americans still held most of the rest of the state.

The British tried again to move up the Hudson River valley in 1779. But the Americans controlled the river from West Point, a key fort about fifty miles north of the city. They blocked the British move.

In western New York, loyalists and Indians attacked American settlers. Washington sent a force to put down the trouble. The fighting continued through 1781. The Americans burned many Iroquois villages. This ended the strength of the Iroquois.

FOCUS ON:

TREASON AT WEST POINT

In the early years of the Revolution, Benedict Arnold was a hero. He led American soldiers to several victories. But Arnold has gone down in history as a traitor.

In 1780, Arnold was put in command of West Point, on the Hudson River. The British could not take this fort by force. But Arnold agreed to sell them the plans to the fort. Arnold gave the plans to British major John André, but the plans never reached the British commanders. André was caught and hanged as a spy. Arnold escaped to a British ship. For the rest of the war, he fought on the British side.

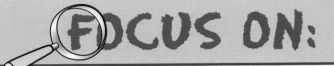

Revolutionary Women

Women were not allowed to be soldiers during the Revolution. Some went to war anyway, disguised as men. Others were cooks, laundresses, and nurses to the Continental army. But even women who stayed home played a big part in the war.

Women raised money for the war. They wove cloth for uniforms. Some women learned to make and repair guns. And with men away fighting, women ran farms and businesses.

Many New York women took brave actions. Catherine Schuyler was one. She set fire to the fields of her farm near Saratoga to keep the British army from taking the crops.

Sibyl Ludington was the daughter of a militia leader in Putnam County. In 1777, word reached her home that the British planned to attack nearby Danbury, Connecticut. Sibyl jumped on her horse and rode through the night to alert her father's troops.

Anna Smith Strong of Long Island was part of a patriot spy ring. She fought the war with her clothesline. To tell other members of the ring where to meet, she would hang a black petticoat, followed by a certain number of handkerchiefs. The British never knew this was a code.

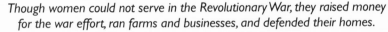

Though women could not serve in the Revolutionary War, they raised money for the war effort, ran farms and businesses, and defended their homes.

This wood engraving shows the triumphant entrance of Washington's army into New York at the end of the Revolutionary War.

In October 1781, British forces surrendered to Washington at Yorktown, Virginia. Independence was won. The war officially ended in 1783, when Britain and the new United States signed a peace treaty.

New York City was the last British **refuge**. Many loyalists had fled there during the war. When the peace treaty was signed, about thirty thousand loyalists packed up and sailed for Canada or Britain.

The last British troops left New York on November 25, and Washington entered the city. On December 4, he said farewell to his officers. The long war was over at last.

CHAPTER REVIEW

1. Where was New York's first Revolutionary War battle fought?
2. What did the Americans do with the guns from Fort Ticonderoga?
3. Where did George Washington go after he left Boston?
4. Why was Saratoga a turning point in the war?
5. Which side held New York City for most of the war?

LEADING THE NATION

With the end of the Revolution, Americans were free. They could form their own government, a **democracy**. They could make their own laws. And New York took a leading role in the new United States.

A NEW GOVERNMENT

New York and the other states were only loosely tied together at first. They were joined by plan of government called the Articles of Confederation. Under the Articles, Congress could not make people pay taxes. It could pass laws, but the states did not have to obey them. States could issue their own money.

All this made it hard to run the country. In 1787, delegates from the states met in Philadelphia to find a better way. They ended up writing a new constitution.

FOCUS ON:

ALEXANDER HAMILTON (1755—1804)

Alexander Hamilton was one of the authors of the U.S. Constitution. Born in the West Indies, he went to New York in 1773. During the Revolutionary War, he was an aide to George Washington.

In 1787, Hamilton was a New York delegate at the Constitutional Convention. He wanted a strong central government. With John Jay of New York and James Madison of Virginia, he wrote a series of essays called *The Federalist* papers. The essays helped win support for the Constitution.

In 1789, Hamilton became the first secretary of the treasury. He was widely admired. But he also had many rivals. One rival was Aaron Burr. In 1804, Burr was running for election as governor of New York. He challenged Hamilton to a duel. The duel took place in Weehawken, New Jersey, on July 11. Hamilton was shot and later died from his wound.

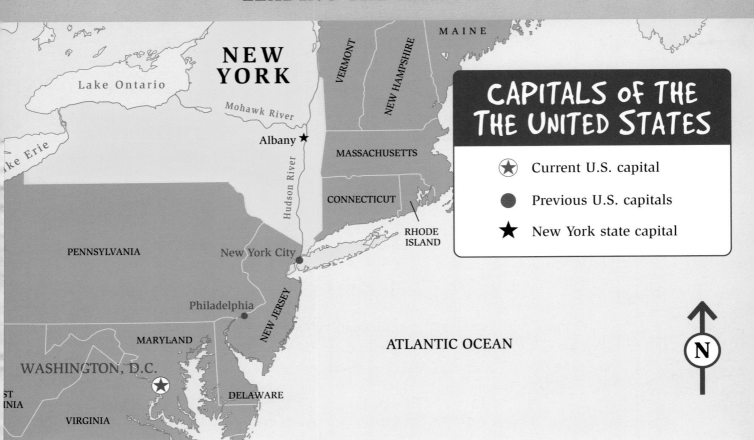

NEW YORK

Lake Ontario

Mohawk River

Albany ★

VERMONT

NEW HAMPSHIRE

MAINE

MASSACHUSETTS

Lake Erie

CONNECTICUT

RHODE ISLAND

PENNSYLVANIA

New York City

Philadelphia

NEW JERSEY

MARYLAND

WASHINGTON, D.C.

DELAWARE

VIRGINIA

ATLANTIC OCEAN

N

CAPITALS OF THE THE UNITED STATES

★ Current U.S. capital

● Previous U.S. capitals

★ New York state capital

The Constitutional **Convention** finished its work in September. Before the new U.S. Constitution could take effect, nine of the thirteen states had to **ratify** (approve) it. New York was the eleventh state to approve the Constitution, on July 26, 1788.

New York City was the first national capital. In April 1789, George Washington was sworn in there as the first president. The national capital later moved to Philadelphia and then to Washington, D.C. Those cities were nearer to the center of the country. Albany became New York's state capital in 1797.

THE ERIE CANAL

In the early 1800s many Americans wanted to move west. There was good land beyond the mountains. But getting there took weeks of travel over terrible roads.

New York governor De Witt Clinton had a better idea. He wanted the state to build a canal all the way from Buffalo, on Lake Erie, to Albany, on the Hudson River. At first people mocked the idea of the canal. It would be almost impossible to build, they said. But Clinton was sure it could be built—and it was.

DID YOU KNOW . . .

Martin Van Buren was the first New Yorker to become president of the United States. He served from 1837 to 1841. Millard Fillmore was the second. Fillmore was vice president under President Zachary Taylor, who died in 1850. Fillmore finished Taylor's term, serving until 1853.

FOCUS ON:

SHIPS IN NEW YORK HARBOR

In the 1840s, New York City's waterfront looked like a forest of bare trees. The "trees" were the tall masts of clipper ships. These swift ships sailed all around the world, carrying people and goods.

The clipper ships helped build U.S. trade with China and other Asian countries. They carried people to California after gold was found there in 1848.

Clippers ruled the seas, but steamboats ruled the rivers. Robert Fulton's steamboat the *Clermont* was tested on the Hudson River in 1807. After that, steamships plied the Hudson and other American rivers. And by 1870, oceangoing steamships were replacing clipper ships.

During the 1800s, New York City's seaport was the busiest in the country, with clipper ships that carried people and goods all over the world.

Clinton opened the canal in 1825 by sailing from Lake Erie to Albany. Then he continued down the Hudson River. At New York City, he dumped two casks of water from Lake Erie into the Atlantic Ocean. That act celebrated the new link between the Great Lakes and the Atlantic.

The Erie Canal made it easy to travel to and from the Great Lakes. It

opened the heart of North America to settlers and trade. It also brought growth to upstate New York. All along the canal route, new towns sprang up. More canals were built to link other parts of the state.

Thousands of people lived and worked along the canals. Canal boat captains often took their families along. Older children

Barges sail along the Erie Canal between the Atlantic Ocean and the Great Lakes.

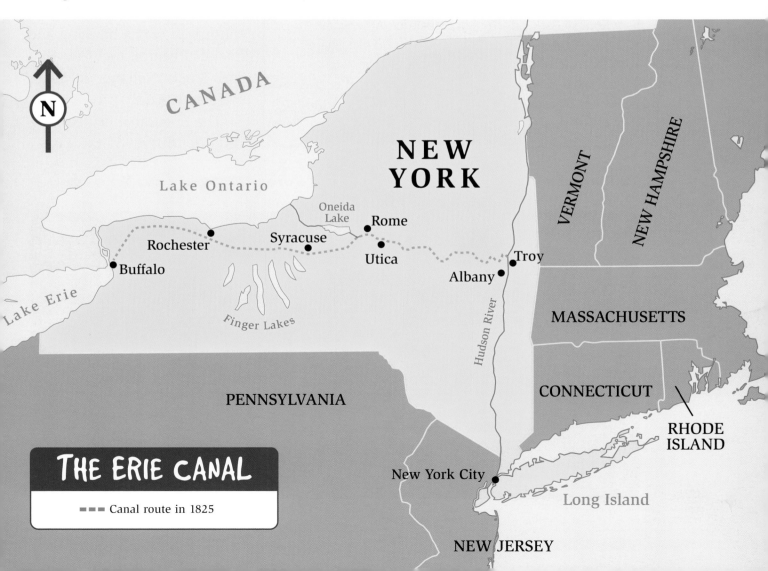

THE ERIE CANAL

- - - Canal route in 1825

THE WAR OF 1812

In 1812, war again broke out between the United States and Britain. There were several reasons for the new war. Britain wanted to keep Americans from trading with its old enemy, France. To accomplish this, sailors on British ships were stopping U.S. ships at sea. They said they were looking for British deserters, but they often removed American sailors and forced them to serve on British naval ships. Britain also helped Indians resist American settlers moving west.

Some battles were fought in New York. In 1814, the British sent an army south from Canada. Their goal was New York City. In September, the Americans stopped the British in a naval battle on Lake Champlain. After that, the British pulled back to Canada.

The war ended with a peace treaty signed in December 1814. Neither side gained anything. But after the war, the United States began a period of great growth.

helped out. Canal boats were towed by mules that walked along towpaths on the shore. Often the children walked alongside the mules to lead them at a steady pace.

NEW YORK CITY GROWS

During the Revolution, two big fires took a toll on New York City. But the city bounced back quickly after the war. Even before the Erie Canal opened, New York City was the busiest port in the country. It was a banking and financial center, too. The New York Stock Exchange formed there in 1792.

The Erie Canal helped New York City thrive. As the gate-

The New York Stock Exchange (pictured here in the late 1800s) opened in 1792, helping to make New York the banking and financial capital of the country.

During the 1800s, tenement buildings housed thousands of people who immigrated to New York City from Europe.

way to the canal, the city was the gateway to the country. People and goods passed through constantly. By 1800, New York City was the largest city in the United States.

But the city was just beginning to grow. Newcomers poured into the city in the 1800s. Many were immigrants from Ireland, which was hit by famine from 1845 to 1850. By 1850, more than half a million people lived in New York. That did not include the population of Brooklyn, which was then a separate town.

SOCIAL CHANGES

During the 1800s, many people moved from farms to towns and cities throughout New York. They found jobs in new mills and factories. New York's factories made bricks, cloth, candles, firearms, and many other products.

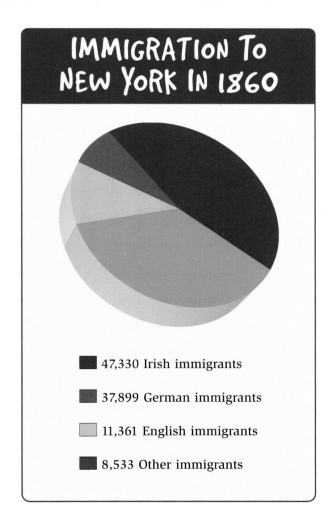

IMMIGRATION TO NEW YORK IN 1860

- 47,330 Irish immigrants
- 37,899 German immigrants
- 11,361 English immigrants
- 8,533 Other immigrants

New York set up public school districts statewide in the early 1800s. Children did not have to go to school, but by the mid-1800s, most children under age fourteen did. They learned basics—reading, writing, spelling, and arithmetic. A number of colleges were also founded in the state at this time.

Schools gave many New Yorkers a chance for better lives. Often, women did not get that chance. In the 1800s, women were not allowed to vote.

They were turned away by colleges. They were barred from most professions. A married woman had no property. Everything belonged to her husband.

Women began to demand fair treatment. Elizabeth Cady Stanton of New York was a leader in this movement. She organized the first woman's rights convention in the United States.

The convention took place in July 1848 at Seneca Falls, New York. The women called for equal rights for men and women. One newspaper called it "the most shocking and unnatural incident ever recorded in the history of womanity."

The fight for woman's rights would last many years. But Americans faced an even bigger problem in the 1800s. That problem was slavery.

Elizabeth Cady Stanton helped organize the first woman's rights convention in Seneca Falls, New York.

Elizabeth Cady Stanton and Women's Rights

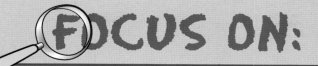

FOCUS ON:

SOJOURNER TRUTH (1797–1883)

Sojourner Truth was born a slave named Isabella, on a farm in Ulster County, New York. In 1827, New York ended slavery. Isabella gained her freedom. She found work as a servant in New York City, and she began to preach on street corners there. She spoke out against slavery and for woman's rights. In 1843, she decided to travel with her message. Taking the name Sojourner Truth, she preached throughout the country. She could not read or write, but she held people spellbound when she spoke. During the Civil War, President Abraham Lincoln invited her to the White House. He gave her a job advising newly freed slaves. After the war, she continued to help freed slaves and to work for woman's rights.

Sojourner Truth, a powerful speaker, traveled the country to encourage equality for all people.

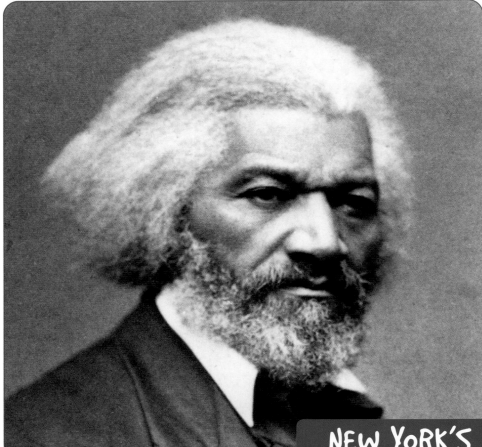

Frederick Douglass was a leader of the abolitionist movement and one of America's first African American voices against racial injustices.

SLAVERY AND THE CIVIL WAR

In 1800, one of every 20 New Yorkers was African American. They included about 21,000 slaves and about 10,000 free blacks. The last slaves were freed by law in 1827.

Life was often hard for freed blacks. They faced **discrimination**. But many were helped by **abolitionists**, people who were against slavery. New York was a center for the abolitionists. Frederick Douglass, a

NEW YORK'S AFRICAN AMERICAN POPULATION VS. OTHERS—1800

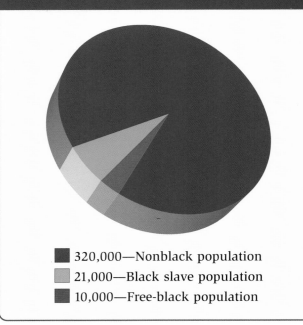

■ 320,000—Nonblack population
■ 21,000—Black slave population
■ 10,000—Free-black population

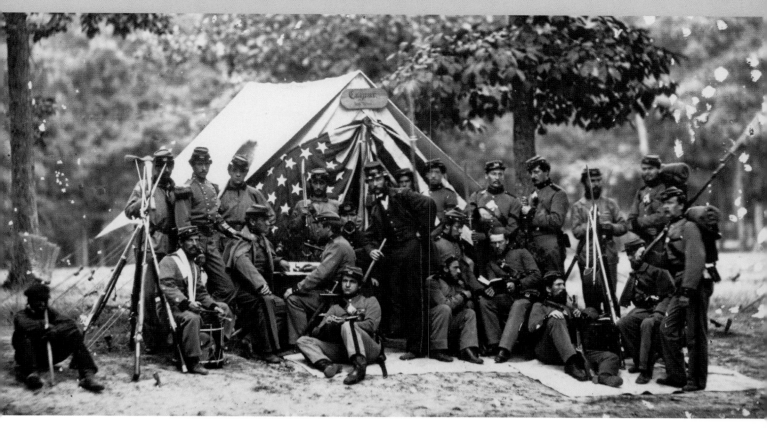

The 8th New York State militia troops shown in this photograph fought among thousands of New Yorkers in the Union army during the Civil War.

leader of the fight against slavery, lived in Rochester. Many New Yorkers helped slaves escape through the Underground Railroad. This network of safe houses guided slaves from the Southern states to freedom in Canada.

The Civil War began in April 1861, after several Southern states left the Union. There were no battles in New York. But no state sent more troops and supplies to the Union army than New York.

The state's industries grew as they turned out goods for the war. When the war finally ended in 1865, New York was ready for another growth spurt.

CHAPTER REVIEW

1. When did New York approve the Constitution?
2. Whose idea was the Erie Canal?
3. What did the Erie Canal do for New York City?
4. What was the goal of the women who met at Seneca Falls in 1848?
5. Who was Frederick Douglass?

UNIT 6 | CITIES AND INDUSTRIES

New York grew rapidly after the Civil War. Railroads spread across the state. Factories sprang up. New York's national role grew as well. New Yorkers were leaders in politics, business, the arts, and many other fields.

RAILROADS AND ROBBER BARONS

By the 1860s, railroads linked New York's major cities and towns, and they linked New York to the rest of the country. Railroads changed the way people lived and did business.

Railroads made it easy to ship goods. Trains were faster and cheaper than canal barges. This helped industries grow throughout the state. New York factories made everything from steel to shirt collars.

By the late 1800s, railroads shipped goods from New York all over the country.

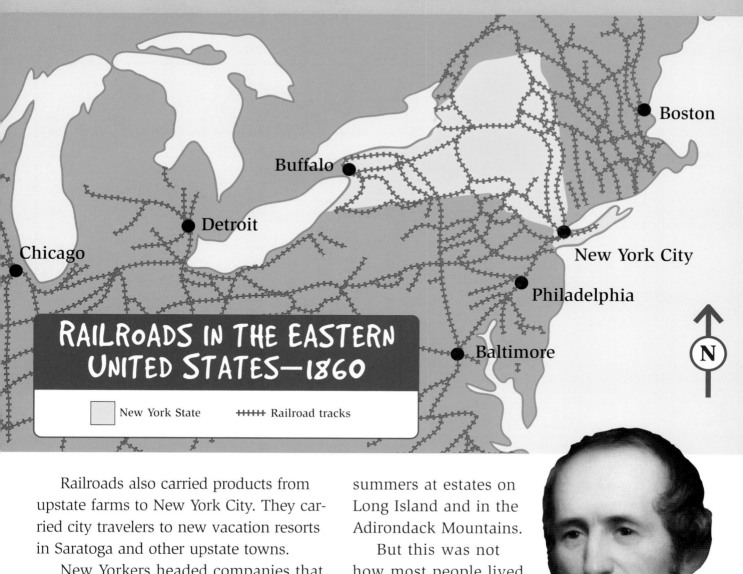

RAILROADS IN THE EASTERN
UNITED STATES—1860

Boston

Buffalo

Detroit

Chicago

New York City

Philadelphia

Baltimore

N

New York State   ┼┼┼┼┼ Railroad tracks

Railroads also carried products from upstate farms to New York City. They carried city travelers to new vacation resorts in Saratoga and other upstate towns.

New Yorkers headed companies that built some of the country's big national railways. The growth of railroads and industry made some of these businessmen very wealthy. They were known as "robber barons" because they got rich through ruthless deals.

New Yorkers such as Jay Gould, Cornelius Vanderbilt, and John D. Rockefeller built huge fortunes. They headed big companies that controlled the railroads, the oil industry, and other industries.

The wealthy lived well. They built mansions in New York City. They spent summers at estates on Long Island and in the Adirondack Mountains.

But this was not how most people lived. Poverty was a big problem. Life was especially hard for the immigrants who were flocking to New York.

Cornelius Vanderbilt made a huge fortune by controlling railroad, oil, and other industries.

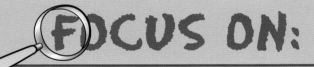
THE ROOSEVELT FAMILY

The Roosevelts are one of New York's oldest families. Three members were national leaders.

Theodore Roosevelt (1858–1919), born in New York City, was president of the United States from 1901 to 1909. He was a popular and colorful figure. Among other things, he led a cavalry regiment, the Rough Riders, in the Spanish-American War. Roosevelt served as governor of New York and then as vice president before becoming president.

Franklin D. Roosevelt (1882–1945), born in Hyde Park, was president of the United States from 1933 to his death in 1945. He was a distant relative of Theodore. He also was governor of New York before becoming president. FDR, as he was called, was crippled by polio in 1921, but he did not let that end his career. As president, he led the country through two great crises, the Great Depression and World War II.

Eleanor Roosevelt (1884–1962) worked for human rights and world peace. She was Theodore's niece. She married Franklin, who was her distant cousin. Eleanor was the busiest first lady in U.S. history. She had her own radio program and newspaper column. She spoke out for the rights of African Americans, women, and the poor. After Franklin's death, she became a U.S. delegate to the United Nations.

President Franklin Roosevelt and his wife, Eleanor, belonged to one of New York's oldest families.

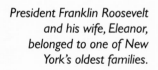

IMMIGRATION

In 1870, almost 1 million people lived in New York City. Nearly four out of ten had been born in another country. And more immigrants were on the way. Over the next 50 years, a great wave of people poured into the United States from Europe. About 17 million arrived in New York.

The Irish had been the biggest immigrant group. Now people from Germany, Italy, eastern Europe, and other areas came. The newcomers wanted freedom and a chance to make a living. As the country's busiest port, New York City was their gateway to a better life.

The Statue of Liberty, a gift from France, stood for the promise of the new land. It was placed in New York Harbor in 1886.

In 1892, Ellis Island, also in New York Harbor, became the entry point for immigrants to the United States. There, U.S. officials screened the new arrivals. Many newcomers traveled on to other parts of the country. But others stayed in New York.

New York City saw the biggest growth. It was a true melting pot, mixing cultures from many nations. But immigrants settled in other parts of the state, too. By 1900, one of every five people in western New York had been born in another country.

These immigrants are among thousands who journeyed through Ellis Island when they arrived in America.

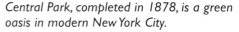

Central Park, completed in 1878, is a green oasis in modern New York City.

GROWING PAINS

As more people arrived, New York City grew crowded. Streets and buildings spread north on Manhattan. To keep some open space, the city set aside more than eight hundred acres (3.24 sq km) for what became Central Park. **Aqueducts** were built to carry water to the city from reservoirs upstate.

Public works like these helped the city grow. But they also brought dishonesty. William H. Tweed became the commissioner of public works in 1870. "Boss" Tweed headed Tammany Hall, a **corrupt** political group.

Tweed and his ring cheated the

Since 1886, when France presented it to the United States, the Statue of Liberty has been a symbol of liberty, democracy, and freedom.

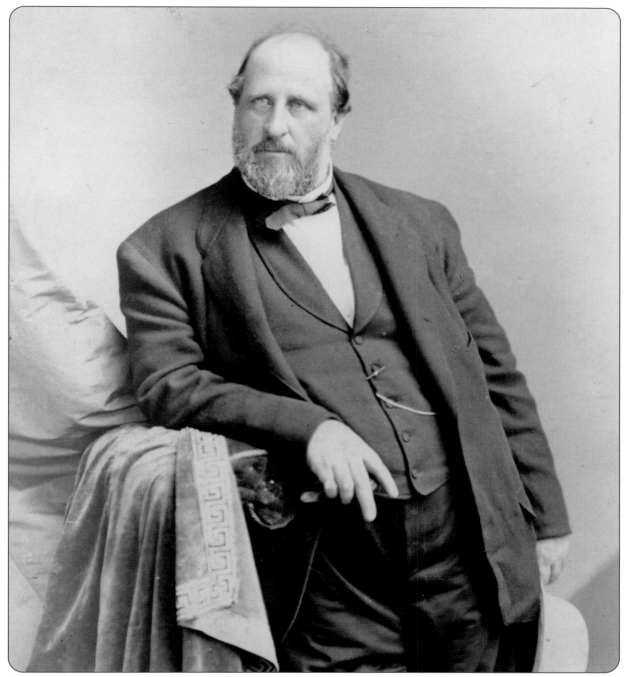

Public works commissioner William "Boss" Tweed and his gang got rich as they cheated the city of New York out of millions of dollars.

city out of millions of dollars. In one case, he bought three hundred benches for five dollars each. Then he sold the benches to the city for six hundred dollars each. Newspapers finally uncovered Tweed's crimes. He went to jail.

Slowly, the city spread outward from Manhattan. The Brooklyn Bridge was built to link Manhattan and Brooklyn. When the bridge opened in 1883, it was the marvel of its day.

FOCUS ON:

SUSAN B. ANTHONY (1820—1906)

A shocking event took place in Rochester, New York, on election day in 1872. Fourteen women tried to vote. They were arrested. Women were not allowed to vote in 1872.

One of those women was Susan B. Anthony. Anthony was a leader of the women's movement. She was born in Massachusetts and moved to New York with her family at age six.

Anthony became a schoolteacher in upstate New York. There she met Elizabeth Cady Stanton and joined the fight for woman's rights. Suffrage—the right to vote—was her main cause. With Stanton, she formed the National Woman Suffrage Association (NWSA) in 1869.

Anthony worked tirelessly for her cause. She wrote articles and gave speeches. She organized meetings and rallies. She did not live to see women vote. Women finally won the right to vote in 1920, with the Nineteenth **Amendment** to the Constitution.

Susan B. Anthony became one of the strongest voices in the fight for women's right to vote.

How did the Brooklyn Bridge change New York City?

In 1894, Queens and Staten Island joined New York City. Brooklyn joined in 1898, making New York the second largest city in the world, after London. More than 3 million people lived in the city.

SWEATSHOPS

Most immigrants had to take low paying jobs. They worked in factories and as servants. Many worked in **sweatshops**. These small, crowded workrooms turned out clothing and many other products. Sweatshops were crammed into basements and lofts all over New York City.

Men, women, and even young children took jobs in sweatshops. They worked six days a week, twelve hours a day. Often they earned no more than one dollar a day. Many workrooms were dark and crowded. Sometimes employers locked the workers in until their work was done.

For New York's poorest, living conditions were terrible. They lived in **tenements**, where six people might share a single dark room. An entire building might share a sink. In crowded tenements, diseases spread quickly.

Reformers called for change. Workers began to form **unions** and fight for better wages and working conditions. Through private and public efforts, the poor began to get better health care and education.

In March 1911, a fire broke out at the Triangle Shirtwaist Factory in New York City. The fire killed 146 workers, mostly women and girls. After that tragedy, new safety and child labor laws were passed.

After a huge fire killed 146 people and left the Triangle Shirtwaist Factory in ruins, new child labor and safety laws were enacted to protect workers.

NEW YORK IN A NEW CENTURY

In the early 1900s, most New Yorkers were not as rich as the "robber barons." Nor were they as poor as the sweatshop workers. They were middle-class families. Most lived in cities or in the suburbs that were starting to grow up around cities. Only about one of four New Yorkers lived in the countryside.

Inventions like the telephone and electric lights were changing the way

THE KODAK CAMERA

New York inventor George Eastman made photography a hobby for everyone. Before 1885, photographs were taken with big, heavy cameras that used glass plates. Eastman came up with flexible rolled film. In 1888, he began to sell a simple box camera. He called it a Kodak.

The Kodak slogan was "You press the button, we do the rest." The camera came loaded with film. When people had used the film, they sent the whole camera back to the factory in Rochester. There, the pictures were developed, and the camera was loaded with fresh film.

Kodak NO. 1 held enough film for one hundred pictures. When all the pictures were shot, the whole camera was returned to the factory for processing.

By the early 1900s, traffic in both the cities and in the country were busy enough to make New York the first state to set speed limits for automobiles.

people lived. Automobiles were taking over the roads. In 1904, New York was the first state to have speed limits for automobiles. The limit was ten miles (16 km) per hour in cities and twenty miles (32 km) per hour in open country.

World events shaped New York in the 1900s. World War I (1914–1918)

DID YOU KNOW . . .

New Yorkers saw their first motion picture in 1896, at Koster and Bial's Music Hall in New York City.

stopped the flow of immigrants from Europe to America. Factory owners who needed workers looked to the south. Many African Americans moved from the south to take jobs in New York factories.

Good times followed World War I. But the 1920s ended with the crash of the New York Stock Exchange in October 1929. Many people lost their savings when stock prices dropped. New York was hard hit in the **economic depression** that followed the crash. Businesses closed. People lost their jobs.

The economy picked up after the United States entered World War II

HARLEM

In the early 1900s, thousands of African Americans left the South for cities in the North. They hoped to find a better life. In New York, many African Americans settled in Harlem, in northern Manhattan.

Harlem grew into one of the largest black communities in the United States. In the 1920s, it became a center of African American culture. Writers, artists, musicians, and political leaders were part of the Harlem scene. This movement was called the Harlem Renaissance. *Renaissance* means "rebirth."

Musicians, as well as artists and writers, helped make Harlem the center of African American culture in the 1920s.

The headquarters of the United Nations are located in New York City.

in 1941. New York factories made goods for the war. New York City hummed with activity as troops shipped out to fight in Europe.

After the war, New York City took on a new international role. In 1952, it became the site of headquarters of the new United Nations.

CHAPTER REVIEW

1. Why were some businessmen of the 1800s called "robber barons"?
2. What country sent the Statue of Liberty to the United States?
3. How did New York City provide water for its growing population?
4. How many hours did sweatshop workers work in a day?
5. Where did most New Yorkers live in the early 1900s?

MODERN NEW YORK

The last fifty years have brought changes and challenges to New York. One big change is the growth of suburbs. Many people have moved out of city centers to nearby towns. New houses, shopping centers, and highways ring the cities today.

NEW YORK'S PEOPLE

About 19 million people live in New York. The state ranks third in population behind California and Texas. More than four out of five New Yorkers live in cities and suburbs, and more than 8 million live in New

New Yorkers are made up of people from all walks of life.

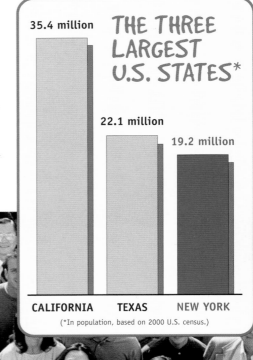

THE THREE LARGEST U.S. STATES*

35.4 million

22.1 million

19.2 million

CALIFORNIA   TEXAS   NEW YORK

(*In population, based on 2000 U.S. census.)

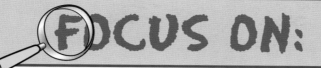

FOCUS ON:

COLIN POWELL
(1937—)

Colin Powell, born in New York City, is the first African American to serve as U.S. secretary of state. He is the son of Jamaican immigrants. Powell joined the U.S. Army as an officer after college. He served in Vietnam in the 1960s and earned eleven medals. After the war, he rose steadily through the army ranks.

In 1989, under President George H.W. Bush, he became chairman of the Joint Chiefs of Staff—the nation's top military officer. He directed U.S. forces in the 1991 Persian Gulf War against Iraq.

Powell retired from the army in 1993. In 2001, President George W. Bush named him secretary of state. In this important post, he helped shape U.S. foreign policy.

Colin Powell is the first African American to serve as U.S. secretary of state.

York City. Buffalo is the state's second largest city. Rochester is third.

New York is still a gateway to the United States. New immigrants have arrived from Latin America and the

How are today's immigrants different from those of the 1800s?

Caribbean, including Cuba. Many others have come from Asian countries—China, Japan, Vietnam, India, and Pakistan. Still others have come from Russia and other parts of the former Soviet Union.

Today African Americans make up about 16 percent of New Yorkers. About 15 percent are Hispanic. More than 5 percent are Asian Americans. American Indians make up less than half a percent of the people. Many American Indians live on **reservations** in upstate New York and eastern Long Island.

WHERE PEOPLE WORK

Most New Yorkers work in service industries. These are industries, such as banking, that provide services rather than making goods.

New York City is the business capital of the country. It is a still a center for trade of all kinds. Advertising, banking, broadcasting, insurance, publishing, and tourism are major industries, too. As the home of the New York Stock Exchange, the city is one of the world's most important financial centers.

Like many northern states, New York has lost factory jobs since the 1960s. But manufacturing is still important. Parts of New York are known for certain products. Glass is made in Corning. Rochester is famous for cameras and film. Statewide, products include computers, scientific instruments, machinery, chemicals, and processed foods.

A fifth of New York's residents live in rural areas.

DID YOU KNOW . . .

More than fifty of the biggest U.S. corporations have their headquarters in New York.

New York has only one-fifth of the farms it had one hundred years ago. Milk is the state's leading farm product. New York farms also produce eggs, apples and other fruits, corn, hay, vegetables, garden plants, maple syrup, and wine.

Like farming, mining is not as important as it once was. But New York still produces garnet, talc, zinc, salt, and other minerals.

FOCUS ON:

STATE GOVERNMENT

New York's state government is modeled on the federal government of the United States. It has three branches.

The legislative branch makes laws. New York's legislature has two houses, the **Assembly** and the Senate. The members are elected every two years.

The executive branch carries out the laws. It is headed by the governor. Voters choose the governor every four years.

The judicial branch interprets laws and applies them in court cases. This branch is made up of the courts. The highest court is the New York Court of Appeals. The governor picks the seven judges on this court. They serve for fourteen years.

TRANSPORTATION AND COMMUNICATION

New York is a transportation hub. Planes from around the world come and go at John F. Kennedy International Airport in New York City. The city's La Guardia Airport handles domestic flights. There are half a dozen other large airports in the state.

Major highways include the state thruway, which runs from New York City to Buffalo. The main rail lines run through the Hudson and Mohawk river valleys. The St. Lawrence Seaway allows oceangoing ships to travel to the Great Lakes along New York's northern border.

Railroads are still important to New York, but today most freight travels by truck.

FOCUS ON:

SKYSCRAPERS

In the early 1900s, Manhattan was running out of open land. There was only one way to squeeze more offices and apartments onto the island. That was to build taller buildings. Two inventions—steel framing and the elevator—made it possible.

New York became famous for its tall buildings, known as skyscrapers. People were amazed by the Singer Building, finished in 1908. At 612 feet (187 m), it was the tallest building in the world—but not for long. New York's skyscrapers reached higher and higher. The Woolworth Building, 40 Wall Street, the Chrysler Building—each in turn held the "tallest building" title.

In 1931, the Empire State Building took the title. At 1,250 feet (381 m), it was more than twice as tall as the old Singer Building. It kept the title until 1972, when the twin towers of the World Trade Center were built.

Since the loss of the towers in 2001, the Empire State Building is once again the tallest building in New York (but not the world). And it is one of the city's most famous landmarks.

For more than forty years the Empire State Building reigned as the tallest building in the world.

A web of roads, railways, tunnels, and bridges links New York City to nearby areas. Millions of people go to work in Manhattan each day by train, bus, car, and ferry. New York City's subway system is one of the world's largest. Its port handles about $90 billion worth of cargo a year.

Major New York newspapers such as the *New York Times* and the *Wall Street Journal* are read around the world. New York is home to more than 250 radio stations and 40 television stations. Three major television networks are based in New York City.

EDUCATION AND CULTURE

The State University of New York (SUNY) has campuses throughout the state. The City University of New York is another large public system. Columbia University is the state's oldest university. It was founded in 1754 as King's College in New York City. There are many other private colleges and universities in the state. Specialty schools range from the Juilliard School (performing arts) in New York City to the U.S. Military Academy at West Point.

New York also has some of the world's best-known museums. The American Museum of Natural History, Metropolitan Museum of Art, and other major museums are in New York City. Upstate museums include the Strong Museum in Rochester and the State Museum in Albany. The National Baseball Hall of Fame is in Cooperstown.

There are public libraries throughout the state. The New York (City) Public Library is one of the largest in the nation.

The Metropolitan Museum of Art is a popular destination for visitors to New York City.

Clouds reflect in the water of a lake in Adirondack State Park, the largest state park in the eastern United States.

FOCUS ON:

RUTH BADER GINSBURG
(1933—)

Ruth Bader Ginsburg, born New York City, is a U.S. Supreme Court justice. When she became a lawyer in 1959, most law firms would not hire a woman. She turned to teaching.

Ginsburg taught law at Columbia University. In the 1970s she became known for her work for woman's rights. She won several important Supreme Court cases. In 1980, she became a federal judge. And in 1993, she became the second woman ever named to the Supreme Court.

Ruth Bader Ginsgurg is seen here as she is sworn in as a U.S Supreme Court justice.

RECREATION

New Yorkers never lack things to do. New York City is famous for music and theater. It has Broadway shows, the Metropolitan Opera, and endless other attractions. Saratoga and other upstate towns have their own performing arts centers.

Ocean beaches on Long Island draw crowds of vacationers each summer. People enjoy hiking and skiing in the mountains and boating and swimming on the state's lakes and rivers. Adirondack State Park is the largest wilderness park in the eastern United States. New York also has the oldest state park in the nation, at Niagara Falls. The falls, shared with Canada, are one of the world's natural wonders.

Fans enjoy all kinds of sports. Buffalo has the Buffalo Bills (football) and the Buffalo Sabres (hockey). New York City has the Yankees and the Mets (baseball), the Knicks (basketball), the Rangers (hockey), and the Giants and the Jets (football).

The state also hosts top-level events in tennis, horse racing, and other sports. Runners from all over the world enter the New York City Marathon each year.

The Jets are one of three professional football teams in New York.

Water flows over Niagara Falls, one of the world's natural wonders.

The twin towers of the World Trade Center in Manhattan were destroyed when terrorists flew airplanes into them on September 11, 2001.

The Statue of Liberty stands as a symbol of strength to New Yorkers as they face the challenges of the future.

MEETING NEW CHALLENGES

New York faces many challenges today. They range from traffic jams to pollution. Where factories have closed, people have struggled to find new jobs. Poverty has led to crime and drug abuse.

Terrorism is a new threat. On September 11, 2001, terrorists flew two hijacked airliners into the twin towers of the World Trade Center in New York City. Nearly three thousand people were killed, and both towers were destroyed.

The attack stunned the world. But New York has bounced back. By 2004, there were plans to rebuild. A new tower—the tallest in the world—would rise at the Trade Center site.

New Yorkers are working hard to meet the challenges that face their state. They are proud of its history. And they look forward to its future.

CHAPTER REVIEW

1. What percent of New Yorkers are Hispanic?
2. In what type of industries do most New Yorkers work?
3. What New York city is famous for cameras and film?
4. What two cities does the state thruway connect?
5. Where is the National Baseball Hall of Fame?

GLOSSARY

abolitionists: People who want to end (abolish) slavery.

amendment: A change, such as a change to the U.S. Constitution.

apprentices: People who learn a skill by working alongside a master.

aqueduct: A channel or pipe that carries water for a long distance.

artisans: Skilled workers who make things with their hands.

assembly: A group of people who come together to make laws and take other actions.

clan: A group of families who share a common ancestor.

colony: A settlement founded and governed by a distant country.

confederacy: A group of tribes or states that join together.

constitution: A plan of government.

convention: A formal meeting held for a specific purpose.

corrupt: Dishonest.

council: A group of people who meet to exchange views and make decisions.

culture: The way of life shared by a group of people. Culture includes language, beliefs, customs, foods, and holidays.

delegates: People sent to speak or act for others.

democracy: A system in which people control the government.

discrimination: Unfair treatment.

economic depression: A severe business slump.

gristmill: A mill where grain is ground into flour.

indentured servants: People who are bound by contract to work for others for a set time.

land bridge: A narrow strip of land joining two larger landmasses.

loyalists: People who remained loyal to the British government during the American Revolution.

militia: A group of citizens called to fight in emergencies.

patriots: People who were against British rule during the American Revolution.

petition: A formal request.

plantation: A large farm growing crops such as tobacco or cotton.

quarter: Provide a place to live.

ratify: Approve.

reformers: People who want to change society for the better.

refuge: A safe place.

representation: Having a voice or say in government.

reservations: Areas set aside for certain groups, such as American Indian tribes.

sachems: Leaders of some American Indian tribes.

sawmill: A mill where lumber is cut.

sweatshops: Small crowded workrooms where low-paid workers put in long hours.

tenements: Crowded, rundown buildings where many families lived in cramped apartments.

unions: Labor organizations that campaign for workers' rights.

Colonial New Yorkers called the British soldiers red coats because of their traditional uniforms.

FOR MORE INFORMATION

Books

Nathan Aaseng, *The Crash of 1929*. San Diego, CA: Lucent Books, 2001.

Deborah Bachrach, *Margaret Sanger*. San Diego, CA: Lucent Books, 1993.

James A. Banks et al., *New York: Adventures in Time and Place*. Carlsbad, CA: SRA/McGraw-Hill, 1998.

James Barter, *Jonas Salk*. San Diego, CA: Lucent Books, 2002.

Lydia Bjornlund, *The Iroquois*. San Diego, CA: Lucent Books, 2001.

Barbara Lee Bloom *The Chinese Americans*. San Diego, CA: Lucent Books, 2002.

Peter Brooke-Ball, *George Eastman: Photography Pioneer*. San Diego, CA: Blackbirch Press, 2004.

Rick Burke, *Theodore Roosevelt*. Chicago: Heinemann Library, 2003.

Andrew Coe and the New York City Fire Museum, eds., *FDNY: An Illustrated History of the Fire Department of New York*. New York: W.W. Norton, 2003.

Ellen Greenman Coffey, *John D. Rockefeller: Richest Man Ever*. San Diego, CA: Blackbirch Press, 2001.

Craig A. Doherty and Katherine M. Doherty, *The Empire State Building*. San Diego, CA: Blackbirch Press, 1998.

———, *The Erie Canal*. San Diego, CA: Blackbirch Press, 1997.

———, *The Statue of Liberty*. San Diego, CA: Blackbirch Press, 1997.

Russell Freedman, *Immigrant Kids*. New York: Penguin-Putnam Books for Young Readers, 1995.

John F. Grabowski, *The New York Rangers*. San Diego, CA: Lucent Books, 2003.

———, *The New York Yankees*. San Diego, CA: Lucent Books, 2002.

Linda Granfield, *97 Orchard Street, New York: Stories of Immigrant Life*. Toronto: Tundra Books, 2001.

James Haskins et al., *Black Stars of the Harlem Renaissance*. Hoboken, NJ: John Wiley & Sons, 2002.

Karen Price Hossell, *The Irish Americans*. San Diego, CA: Lucent Books, 2002.

Claude Hurwicz, *Henry Hudson*. New York: Powerkids Press, 2003.

Scott Ingram, *The Battle of Long Island*. San Diego, CA: Blackbirch Press, 2004.

Susan Johnson, *Boss Tweed and Tammany Hall*. San Diego, CA: Blackbirch Press, 2002.

Stuart A. Kallen and P.M. Boekhoff, *New York*. San Diego, CA: KidHaven Press, 2002.

David C. King, *Benedict Arnold and the American Revolution*. San Diego, CA: Blackbirch Press, 1999.

L.J. Krizner, *Peter Stuyvesant: New Amsterdam and the Origins of New York*. New York: Powerkids Press, 2002.

Janey Levy, *The Erie Canal: A Primary Source History of the Canal That Changed America*. New York: Rosen, 2003.

Loree Lough, *Nathan Hale*. Langhorne, PA: Chelsea House, 2000.

Nancy Louis, *Ground Zero*. Edina, MN: Abdo & Daughters, 2002.

Meg Greene Malvasi, *The Russian Americans*. San Diego, CA: Lucent Books, 2002.

Joanne Mattern, *The Travels of Henry Hudson*. Austin, TX: Raintree Steck-Vaughn, 2000.

Pat McKissack et al., *Sojourner Truth: Ain't I A Woman*. New York: Scholastic, 1994.

Tim McNeese, *The New York Subway System*. San Diego, CA: Lucent Books, 1997.

Milton Metzger, *The American Revolutionaries: A History in Their Own Words 1750–1800*. New York: Thomas Y. Crowell, 1987.

Raymond H. Miller, *Michael Jordan*. San Diego, CA: KidHaven Press, 2003.

David M. Oestreicher, *The Algonquin of New York*. New York: Powerkids Press, 2003.

Keevil Barbara Parker, *Susan B. Anthony: Daring to Vote*. Brookfield, CT: Millbrook Press, 200.

Elaine Pascoe, *The Brooklyn Bridge*. San Diego, CA: Blackbirch Press, 1999.

Catherine M. Petrini, *The Italian Americans*. San Diego, CA: Lucent Books, 2002.

Renee C. Rebman, *Life on Ellis Island*. San Diego, CA: Lucent Books, 2000.

Marla Felkins Ryan and Linda Schmittroth, eds., *Mohawk*. San Diego, CA: Blackbirch Press, 2002.

Mary Hertz Scarbrough, *The Battle of Harlem Heights*. San Diego, CA: Blackbirch Press, 2004.

Virginia Schomp, *New York*. Tarrytown, NY: Benchmark, 1997.

Liz Sonneborn, *The Cuban Americans*. San Diego, CA: Lucent Books, 2002.

———, *The Iroquois*. Danbury, CT: Franklin Watts, 2002.

Tricia Springstub, *The Vietnamese Americans*. San Diego, CA: Lucent Books, 2002.

James D. Torr, *Primary Sources.* San Diego, CA: Lucent Books, 2002.

Michael V. Uschan, *Franklin D. Roosevelt.* San Diego, CA: Lucent Books, 2002.

Catherine A. Welch, *Frederick Douglass.* Minneapolis, MN: Lerner, 2003.

Melissa Whitcraft, *Wall Street.* Danbury, CT: Childrens Press, 2003.

David Winner, *Eleanor Roosevelt.* San Diego, CA: Blackbirch Press, 2004.

Adam Woog, *Lucille Ball.* San Diego, CA: Lucent Books, 2002.

———, *A Sweatshop During the Industrial Revolution.* San Diego, CA: Lucent Books, 2003.

———, *New York.* San Diego, CA: Lucent Books, 2002.

John F. Wukovits, *Colin Powell.* San Diego, CA: Lucent Books, 2000.

Tony Zulo, *The Japanese Americans.* San Diego, CA: Lucent Books, 2002.

CD-ROMs

Animated Atlas: The Revolutionary War. SVE/Churchill, 1999.

Life in Colonial America. Queue, 1996.

Videos

The Brooklyn Bridge (Ken Burns' America). Warner Home Video, 1995.

Ellis Island. A&E Home Video. 2003.

New York: A Documentary Film Collection (set of six films). PBS Home Video. 1999.

The Statue of Liberty (Ken Burns' America). Warner Home Video, 1995.

Web Sites

Adirondack History Network (www.adirondackhistory. org). This Web site, developed by the Adirondack Museum at Blue Mountain Lake, New York, to aid in the study of state and local history, has primary sources, historical records, and other information.

American Journeys (www.americanjourneys.org). Eyewitness accounts of North American exploration.

Battle of Saratoga (www.battle1777.saratoga.org). Historical information about the Battle of Saratoga and about an annual reenactment of the battle.

Brooklyn Bridge (www.endex.com/gf/buildings/bbridge/ bbridge.html): Facts, history, and other information about the Brooklyn Bridge.

Central New York Freedom Trail (www.nyhistory.com/ cnyft). Information about the Underground Railroad in central New York.

Erie Canal Online (www.syracuse.com/features/ eriecanal). Historical and current information about the Erie Canal

Historic Central New York (www.nyhistory.com/central). Biographies of nineteenth-century reformers who lived in central New York.

Historic Hudson Valley (www.hudsonvalley.org). Information about restored historic homes in the Hudson River valley.

Historic Lakes (historiclakes.org). The history of Lake Champlain and Lake George.

I Love New York: New York State for Kids (www. iloveny. com/kids). State facts, games, and other features.

Learning Adventures in Citizenship (www. pbs.org/ wnet/newyork/laic/index.html). The Public Broadcasting System Web companion to *New York: A Documentary Film Collection.*

Long Island: Our Story (www.lihistory.com). Articles, primary sources, and other material on Long Island history from Newsday.

New Netherland Museum (www.newnetherland.org). Information on a replica of Henry Hudson's ship *Half Moon.*

New Netherland Project (www.nnp.org). A virtual tour of New Netherland.

New York Department of State Kids' Room (www. dos.state.ny.us/kidsroom/nysfacts/factmenu.html). State facts and a brief history of New York.

New York State Canals (www.canals.state.ny.us/cculture/ history). Historical and current information about the New York State Canal System.

New York Underground (www.pbs.org/wgbh/amex/ technology/nyunderground). The Public Broadcasting System Web companion to the American Experience episode "New York Underground," about the New York City subway.

Statue of Liberty and Ellis Island: (www.ellisisland.org). This Web site, developed by the Statue of Liberty and Ellis Island, has a searchable database of the names of immigrants who arrived at Ellis Island.

INDEX

DATE DUE

Demco, Inc. 38-293